THE WILD WEST

THE OREGON TRAIL

by Laura K. Murray

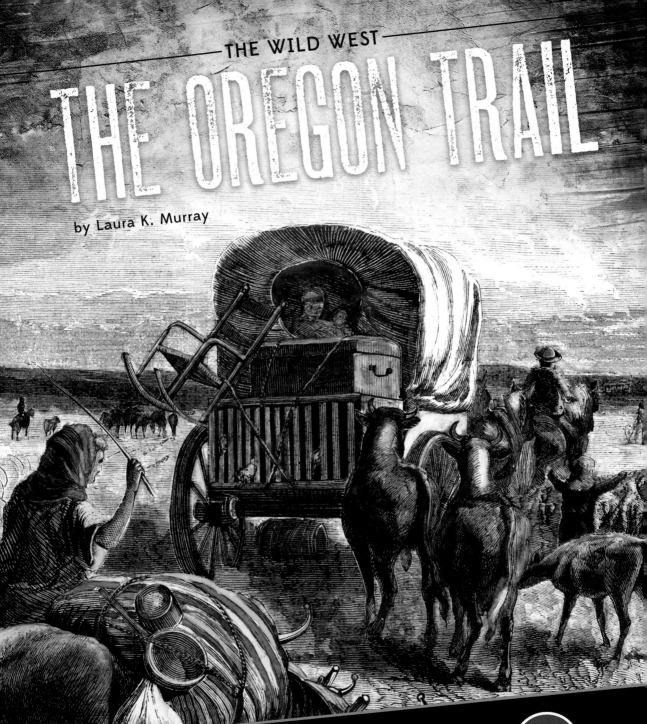

Content Consultant
David Peterson Del Mar
Associate Professor, Department of History
Portland State University

Core Library

An Imprint of Abdo Publishing
abdopublishing.com

abdopublishing.com

Published by Abdo Publishing, a division of ABDO, PO Box 398166, Minneapolis, Minnesota 55439. Copyright © 2017 by Abdo Consulting Group, Inc. International copyrights reserved in all countries. No part of this book may be reproduced in any form without written permission from the publisher. Core Library™ is a trademark and logo of Abdo Publishing.

Printed in the United States of America, North Mankato, Minnesota
032016
092016

THIS BOOK CONTAINS
RECYCLED MATERIALS

Cover Photo: North Wind Picture Archives
Interior Photos: North Wind Picture Archives, 1, 4, 31; Red Line Editorial, 7, 21; Don Troiani/Corbis, 9; Everett Historical/Shutterstock Images, 10; Bettmann/Corbis, 12; DeAgostini/Getty Images, 16; Stocksnapper/Shutterstock Images, 19; AS400 DB/Corbis, 22; MPI/Getty Images, 26, 45; Prisma/UIG/Getty Images, 32; SuperStock, 34; Public Domain, 38; Anton Foltin/Shutterstock Images, 40

Editor: Marie Pearson
Series Designer: Ryan Gale

Cataloging-in-Publication Data
Names: Murray, Laura K., author.
Title: The Oregon Trail / by Laura K. Murray.
Description: Minneapolis, MN : Abdo Publishing, [2017] | Series: The wild West
    | Includes bibliographical references and index.
Identifiers: LCCN 2015960503 | ISBN 9781680782585 (lib. bdg.) |
    ISBN 9781680776690 (ebook)
Subjects: LCSH: Oregon National Historic Trail--Juvenile literature. | Frontier
    and pioneer life ((U.S.)--Juvenile literature. | Pioneers-- Oregon National
    Historic Trail--Social life and customs--Juvenile literature.
Classification: DDC 978/02--dc23
LC record available at http://lccn.loc.gov/2015960503

CONTENTS

CHAPTER ONE

THE CALL OF THE WEST

In the mid-1800s, the West offered Americans a new beginning. It offered land, freedom, adventure, and wealth. During this time, an estimated 300,000 to 500,000 people migrated west. Many sold their farms and packed up their families. They hitched oxen to covered wagons. Thousands headed for a place known as Oregon Country.

Americans headed west in search of new opportunities.

This area did not belong to the United States until 1846. The early pioneers called themselves emigrants. The emigrants' epic route is known today as the Oregon Trail. Until 1869 the Oregon Trail was the main land passage from the Missouri River to the Pacific Coast. The trail stretched approximately 2,100 miles (3,380 km). It cut through the present-day states of Kansas, Nebraska, Wyoming, and Idaho. It ended in western Oregon.

By wagon, the trip took four-and-a-half months or more. Emigrants walked alongside their wagons most of

The Oregon Question

In 1818 the United Kingdom and the United States made an agreement about Oregon Country. People from both nations were allowed to settle there. But there was no clear boundary between British and American land. Citizens of both countries lived in Oregon. The border issue became known as the "Oregon Question." As more Americans moved into Oregon, the United States wanted to settle the question once and for all. The Oregon Treaty of 1846 finally set the northern boundary.

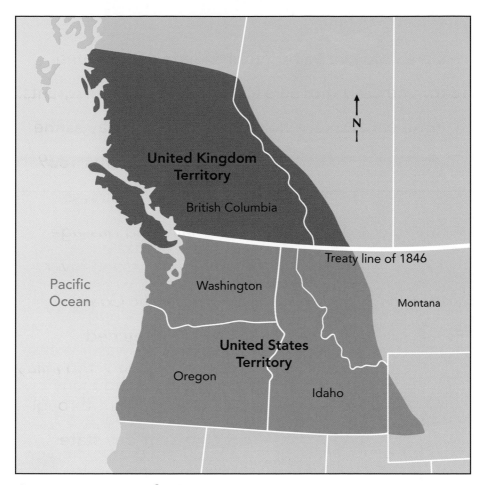

Oregon Treaty of 1846
From 1818 to 1846, both the United States and the United Kingdom had claims on Oregon Country. What do you notice about the treaty line of 1846? How has this influenced borders today?

the way. They crossed plains, prairies, mountains, and deserts. These landscapes were unknown to most of them. But Native Americans had lived in these places for thousands of years.

The Oregon Trail soon became a system of alternate routes and shortcuts. It helped pioneers reach such places as Utah, California, and Montana. The trail opened a new gateway to the West.

A Difficult Journey

The journey along the Oregon Trail was not easy. Emigrants faced many dangers. It is believed 20,000 emigrants died on the trail. They were often buried along the trail or in the trail itself.

Many Native Americans offered emigrants help. They also traded with emigrants. But as more emigrants

Usually Native Americans, including the Shoshones, were friendly to the emigrants.

traveled west, they took land and resources that had belonged to Native Americans. They also spread deadly diseases.

For emigrants, their future lay at the end of the Oregon Trail. The journey to this wild land seemed endless. They traveled one slow step at a time. But they had hopes. Some were drawn by affordable land. Mormons veered toward Utah in search of religious freedom. Others turned south after the discovery of gold in California. For all emigrants, it seemed the western frontier promised a better life. Their adventures along the Oregon Trail and settlement in the West changed the United States forever.

EXPLORING OREGON COUNTRY

In the early 1800s, the United States was acquiring more land. The country nearly doubled in size with the Louisiana Purchase of 1803. The new land included nearly 830,000 square miles (2.2 million sq km) between the Mississippi River and the Rocky Mountains. Americans began exploring this new territory. In 1804 Meriwether Lewis and William Clark led a famous western journey. But their

Americans such as Meriwether Lewis explored the newly purchased land in the West.

Kit Carson was one of many fur trappers and guides during the 1840s.

route to the Pacific Coast was too difficult for families in wagons. One huge obstacle stood in the way: the Rocky Mountains.

In 1812 fur trader Robert Stuart and his group found a 12-mile (19-km)-wide gap through the Rockies. Stuart had heard about the pass from a Shoshone guide. This pass made it possible to travel more safely between the plains and Oregon Country. It was later named the South Pass. It would become an important part of the Oregon Trail. But people did not realize its importance for years. Many people still believed the journey west was far too dangerous for families.

Mountain Men and Missionaries

For several decades, mainly traders and fur trappers explored Oregon Country. They were known as "mountain men." The mountain men began to settle the area. They marked trails and connected paths used by Native Americans. These routes would become parts of the Santa Fe, Oregon, and California trails. Mountain men often formed friendly

A Booming Business

In the early 1800s, the fur trade was booming in Oregon Country. Mountain men trapped beavers and other animals. Then traders sold the pelts to be made into popular fur hats. The trading post Fort Vancouver was built in 1824. Fort Vancouver became one of the final stops on the Oregon Trail. But demand for fur began to decrease in the 1830s. Beavers had become sparse from overhunting. The fur trade declined.

Disease and Violence

Marcus and Narcissa Whitman were missionaries among the Cayuse tribe in present-day Washington. The relationship was tense. The Whitmans did not try to understand Cayuse culture. And the number of emigrants arriving in the West grew. They brought new diseases that killed thousands of Native Americans. The Cayuse became suspicious. In November 1847, a measles outbreak killed many Cayuse children. A group of angry Cayuse killed the Whitmans and 12 other people at the mission. Violence between the Cayuse and whites followed. This became known as the Cayuse War.

relationships with Native Americans. They also established trading posts. In 1834 Nathaniel Wyeth built Fort Hall along the Snake River. It was located in present-day Idaho. Fort Hall became an important stop for early emigrants along the Oregon Trail. Wyeth built another fort in Oregon Country's Willamette Valley. The valley's soil was fertile and good for farming. People began to settle there.

Missionaries were the next to travel west. Reverend Jason Lee set up a mission in Oregon in 1834. Another missionary, Dr. Marcus Whitman, made a trip west in 1836. Whitman's group included his wife, Narcissa, as well as Henry and Eliza Spalding. Narcissa and Eliza became the first white women to cross the Rockies. Their wagon was the first to travel west of Fort Hall. They wanted to teach Christianity to Native Americans. But often missionaries did not try to understand the Native Americans' lifestyles, dress, beliefs, or cultures.

By 1840 wagons were gradually reaching the Willamette Valley. Many more were about to arrive.

EXPLORE ONLINE

Chapter Two talks about early western exploration. The article below has more information about Lewis and Clark's journey. How is the information on the website the same as the information in Chapter Two? What new information did you learn from the website?

Lewis and Clark

mycorelibrary.com/oregon-trail

CHAPTER THREE

OREGON FEVER

Small wagon parties traveled the Oregon Trail in 1840 and 1841. Then, on May 22, 1843, more than 1,000 people in 120 wagons set out for Oregon from Missouri. It was the largest wagon train group to date. It was later called the Great Migration of 1843. Even larger numbers crossed the trail in the following years. The excitement was so widespread that it was known as "Oregon Fever."

Many wagon trains set out to Oregon in the 1840s.

People had many reasons for moving west. But perhaps the biggest draw was free or cheap land. Politicians, missionaries, and newspapers gave glowing reports about Oregon. They promised that it was a land of freedom, happiness, mild weather, and rich soil. These claims were sometimes exaggerated. But that did not stop Oregon Fever from spreading.

Polk Looks West

James Polk was elected president of the United States in 1844. He promised to expand the country's land. At the time, many Americans believed that the United States had a right to expand coast to coast. Polk also helped end the Oregon border dispute with Britain in 1846. Oregon became an official US territory two years later. Oregon Territory included the present-day states of Oregon, Washington, and Idaho, as well as parts of Montana and Wyoming. Oregon became the thirty-third state in 1859.

Starting Out

Families often sold their farms to afford to travel west. Some people worked for their passage. Before starting out on the trail, emigrants made

Emigrants gathered at jumping-off points to prepare their wagons.

their way to "jumping-off" points. These were places along the Missouri River where wagons gathered. They formed groups, called trains, to travel together. One of the most popular jumping-off points was Independence, Missouri. Emigrants camped, met family members, and prepared for the long journey.

Supplies were an important preparation. An average family of four required approximately 1,700 pounds (770 kg) of food. Staples included flour, sugar, salt, bacon, lard, crackers, and coffee. Emigrants also needed cooking utensils, canteens or buckets, rope, tools, seeds, candles, bedding, tents, and other items. They packed farming equipment and toys. They took guns and knives for hunting and protection. Supplies were loaded into the families' wagons. These were usually farm wagons with flat beds and cotton or canvas covers. The wagon would be a family's home on wheels for the next few months.

Most emigrants had teams of oxen pull their wagons. Others used mules. Some also brought along chickens or cows. They waited for the right time to leave. It was important to be on the trail by April or May. That way they would arrive in Oregon before winter. Getting stuck in a snowstorm could be deadly. But leaving too early could mean the animals would not have enough grass to eat along the way.

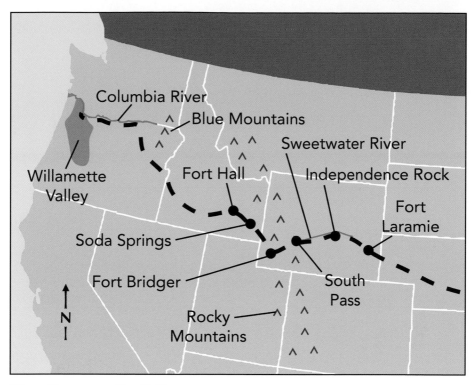

The Oregon Trail Route

This map shows the main route of the Oregon Trail. What rivers, mountains, and landmarks do you notice? Why do you suppose the trail follows this route?

The Route

The exact path of the Oregon Trail varied. But the main trail generally followed major rivers. Water was important for both people and animals. From Independence, emigrants traveled northwest on the prairie of present-day Kansas and Nebraska. They crossed the Platte River and continued along

Fort Laramie was one place emigrants could stop and rest.

the North Platte River. Along the way, they passed landmarks such as Scotts Bluff and Chimney Rock. These landmarks showed travelers they were heading in the right direction.

At Fort Laramie in present-day Wyoming, emigrants could rest, trade, and buy supplies before crossing the Rocky Mountains. Then they traveled 180 miles (290 km) to Independence Rock. They continued along the Sweetwater River to the South Pass in the Rockies. After 1843 many emigrants headed to Wyoming's Fort Bridger on the Green River. They went on to Soda Springs and then Fort Hall on the Snake River. From the desert area, they crossed into the Blue Mountains and arrived at the great Columbia River. They could build rafts and float down the river. Or, after

PERSPECTIVES
The Great American Desert

For much of the 1800s, Americans believed there was an area called the "Great American Desert." Maps and textbooks showed this large, empty area east of the Rockies. It was considered unfit for living. This information was not true. But it had kept people from going west. Explorers and settlers helped change this idea. They showed that people could live in the region. Much of the land was rich in minerals. Settlers learned how to grow crops and raise livestock there. Today the "Great American Desert" is known as the Great Plains. It includes states such as Nebraska, Kansas, and Oklahoma.

1846, they could take Barlow Road over the Cascade Mountains to the Willamette Valley and beyond.

The end of the trail was often considered Oregon City near present-day Portland. But some emigrants stopped earlier, trekked farther, or turned off at other places. And the work was not over once they reached their destination. They would need to find shelter, food, and land to begin their new lives.

On the Oregon Trail, taking a shortcut could turn deadly. Betsey Bayley traveled from Missouri to Oregon in 1845. Her party attempted a new route later named Meek Cutoff. She wrote about the experience in a letter to her sister:

> We had men out in every direction in search of water. They traveled forty or fifty miles [64 or 80 km] in search of water, but found none. You cannot imagine how we all felt. Go back we could not, and we knew not what was before us. Our provisions were failing us. There was sorrow and dismay depicted on every countenance. We were like mariners lost at sea, and in this mountainous wilderness we had to remain for five days. At last we concluded to take a northwesterly direction, and soon the joyful news sounded through the caravan that the advance guard had come to water.

> Source: Kenneth L. Holmes, ed. Covered Wagon Women: Diaries & Letters from the Western Trails 1840–1849. Vol. 1. Glendale, CA: A. H. Clark, 1983. 35–36. Print.

Consider Your Audience

Adapt this passage for a different audience, such as your principal or friends. Write a blog post sharing this same information for the new audience. How does your post differ from the original text, and why?

CHAPTER FOUR

LIFE ON THE TRAIL

Days began early on the Oregon Trail. Emigrants awoke at dawn. They rounded up their animals and started fires. Breakfast was often coffee, beans, and bread. Then the emigrants hitched the oxen to the wagons. They began the day's long march by 7:00 a.m. It was slow. Wagons traveled just 3 miles (4.8 km) per hour. They covered approximately 15 miles (24 km) a day.

Emigrants started their travel early every day. It was a slow journey.

American Bison

American bison along the Oregon Trail amazed emigrants. An estimated 30 to 60 million bison once existed in North America. These shaggy beasts roamed the plains in huge herds. But they were overhunted in the 1800s. Their populations greatly declined. Later efforts to restore bison populations helped improve their numbers. Today large bison herds can be found in Yellowstone National Park.

Most emigrants walked beside the wagons. Riding inside was uncomfortable. It also added weight to the animals' load. Men kept the wagon wheels greased. They waterproofed the canvas with paint or oil. Women and children collected dry bison droppings, called buffalo chips. The chips were used as fire fuel. Emigrants hunted, fished, and gathered berries.

The wagons stopped for a quick noon meal of cold or dry food before continuing. Emigrants needed to be creative to cross rough terrain. They used ropes as a pulley system to get the wagons down steep hills or across rivers. Other times they floated wagons across the water.

At their evening campsite, emigrants formed a large circle with their wagons. Supper usually included bacon or bison meat, bread, and coffee. Then the emigrants visited, played music, and told stories around the fires. Women sewed and did other chores. Emigrants went to bed under the stars, sleeping in tents or wagons. Others stretched out on the ground.

PERSPECTIVES
Women at Work

Some historians suggest that life on the Oregon Trail was more difficult for women than for men. Women's work never ended. Their jobs included taking care of the children, cooking, carrying water, washing, and mending. Some even learned to bake pies over hot rocks. But women also drove ox teams. They often had to get up an hour before everyone else, around 4:00 a.m. Many women experienced another hardship: childbirth. Being pregnant made the long journey even more difficult. But there was no time to rest on the trail.

Danger Ahead

Disease was the most common cause of death on the Oregon Trail. Many emigrants died from cholera. Others suffered smallpox, measles, whooping cough, and other sicknesses. There were few opportunities for bathing and washing on the trail. Emigrants did not always have enough healthy food or clean water.

Accidents were another problem. Some emigrants were not experienced with guns, wagons, or animals. They sometimes shot themselves or others by accident. Some drowned at river crossings. Children were run over by wagon wheels. Weather could be dangerous too. Travelers could not escape lightning, hail, dust, heat, or tornadoes. Heavy rains could cause raging rivers and flooding.

Meeting Native Americans

One of the emigrants' concerns was Native American attacks. But there was violence on both sides. From 1840 to 1860, Native Americans killed approximately 360 emigrants. This was only a fraction of the

Storms were one of many threats on the Oregon Trail.

200,000 emigrants who used the trail. And at the same time, emigrants killed 426 Native Americans.

Attacks were not as common as people thought. Many Native Americans and pioneers traded with one another. The Shoshones and other tribes offered items such as bison robes, moccasins, and salmon. In exchange, emigrants gave them clothing, knives,

The Dakota helped emigrants across rivers.

and food. Other Native Americans acted as guides or
helped at river crossings. They rowed the emigrants'
supplies across the river in canoes. The Dakotas
helped swim animals across the Platte and Laramie
Rivers. But as more settlers arrived, Native Americans
saw their way of life change greatly. This led to
increased conflict.

There was some violence between Native Americans and emigrants on the trail. But many emigrants and Native Americans had positive encounters. Washington Smith Gilliam traveled the Oregon Trail in 1844. He later recalled his experience with Native Americans along the Snake River:

> I can most emphatically say that their treatment of us was of the most friendly kind. They seemed to welcome us, and I think regarded us as curiosities. Anything we possessed was of value to them. For a pin or a rag we could buy a large salmon. When we came to the first crossing of Snake river they volunteered their assistance to us. It was a dangerous crossing, deep, swift and the bar upon which we crossed somewhat narrow. A man had been drowned the previous season by getting off into deep water. . . . They performed their task faithfully, and took us over safely, for which we felt very grateful.

Source: "Reminiscences of Washington Smith Gilliam." Transactions of the 25th Annual Reunion of the Oregon Pioneer Association. Portland: George H. Himes, 1898. 206. Google Play file. Accessed September 29, 2015.

Back It Up

The author of this passage is using evidence to support a point. Write a paragraph describing the point the author is making. Then write down two or three pieces of evidence the author uses to make the point.

A CHANGING TRAIL

Over the years, the trail became a network of worn wagon roads. It became easier to travel. Ferries and bridges were built, as were more forts and trading posts. Thousands of emigrants streamed into Oregon each year. Between 1843 and 1845, the population of Willamette Valley grew from 1,500 to 6,000.

Up to 500,000 emigrants used the Oregon Trail from 1841 to 1884.

Other types of travelers began using the Oregon Trail. Mormons came from Illinois, where they had experienced violence because of their religion. Led by a man named Brigham Young, Mormons turned south off the trail at Fort Bridger. In 1847 they arrived in Utah Territory near the Great Salt Lake. Thousands of Mormons made their home in Utah in the years that followed.

Then, in 1848, gold was discovered in California. Gold seekers rushed west. But they were more interested in gaining riches than

Reminders of the Past

Oregon Trail emigrants left their mark on history. But they also left marks we can see. Approximately 300 miles (483 km) of ruts from emigrants' wagon wheels remain. They are visible in parts of the Oregon National Historic Trail. As emigrants passed Independence Rock, many marked their names on the towering granite formation. Visitors to Wyoming's Independence Rock Historic Site can see those markings today. In addition emigrants left behind diaries and other accounts of daily life on the trail.

in settling land. From 1849 to 1860, nearly 280,000 emigrants headed west. Most of them were bound for California.

Oregon was growing quickly too. Congress passed the Donation Land Claim Act of 1850 (also called the Oregon Land Law). This allowed settlers to claim large pieces of land for free. The settlers were required to live on and work the land for four years. Other land claim laws followed, which helped encourage western settlement. In 1850 Oregon's population was around 12,000. It grew to more than 170,000 by 1880.

Decline of the Trail

In some ways, the trail was safer in its later years. It was more built up and better marked. More people had settled along the way. Mail service along the trail improved communication. But the trail was also more crowded. Overgrazed grass made feeding animals difficult. The trail itself was littered with furniture and discarded junk from overpacked wagons. Graves

Ruts from emigrants' wagon wheels can still be seen today.

and animal bones were scattered along the trail too. They were solemn reminders of those whose journeys had been cut short.

As more people used the trail, tensions between Native Americans and emigrants increased. Emigrants took land and resources that had belonged to

Native Americans. Many settlers treated the Native Americans unfairly. The groups clashed throughout the country. So the US government sent troops and built forts. They forced Native Americans off the lands to make way for settlers. Migration on the trail decreased for a time because of this violence.

Other changes on the Oregon Trail had to do with transportation. People began to use stagecoaches and steamboats to travel west. The transcontinental

PERSPECTIVES
Legends of the Trail

The Oregon Trail has become a legendary part of American history. The story of the emigrants' long and dangerous journey is exciting. But it is also complicated. It sometimes ignores how western settlement affected the lives of Native Americans. Historian Will Bagley writes, "When the era began, every acre of land between the Kansas River and the Pacific Crest belonged to Indian peoples. When it ended three decades later, they owned almost none of it." Many historians today are working to tell the stories of Native Americans and others who played important roles in American history.

Landmarks along the Oregon Trail, such as Independence Rock, can still be visited today.

railroad was built in 1869. It ran from Nebraska to California. This marked the decline of the trail. Travelers could now travel west much more quickly. But people continued using the trail into the 1880s and beyond.

Bringing the Trail to Life

Emigrants such as Ezra Meeker made sure the Oregon Trail was not forgotten. At the age of 76, Meeker retraced the route his family had taken in 1852. He marked the trail and raised funds to preserve it. In 1978 Congress established the Oregon National Historic Trail. Visitors today can experience landmarks, monuments, and historical sites along the trail.

People continue to learn about the ordinary men, women, and children who set out on an extraordinary journey to the Wild West. Their migration west was filled with challenges, sadness, adventure, and triumph. Emigrants played an important role in the history—and future—of the United States.

FURTHER EVIDENCE

Chapter Five included information about the changes of the Oregon Trail. What is one of the main points of this chapter? What evidence is used to support this point? Read the article at the website below. Then find a quote from the website that supports the chapter's main point. Does the website present new evidence?

Historic Wagon Ruts
mycorelibrary.com/oregon-trail

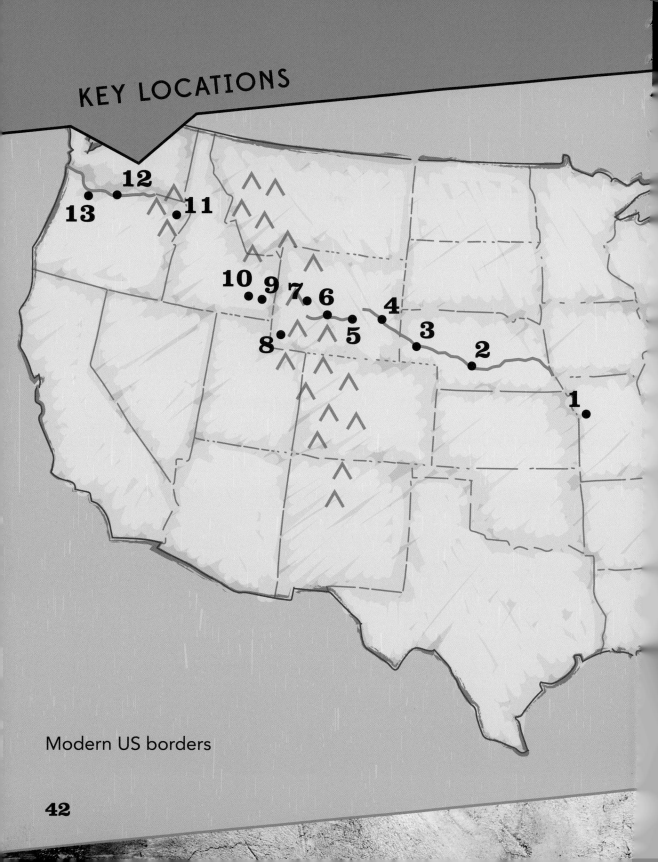

Modern US borders

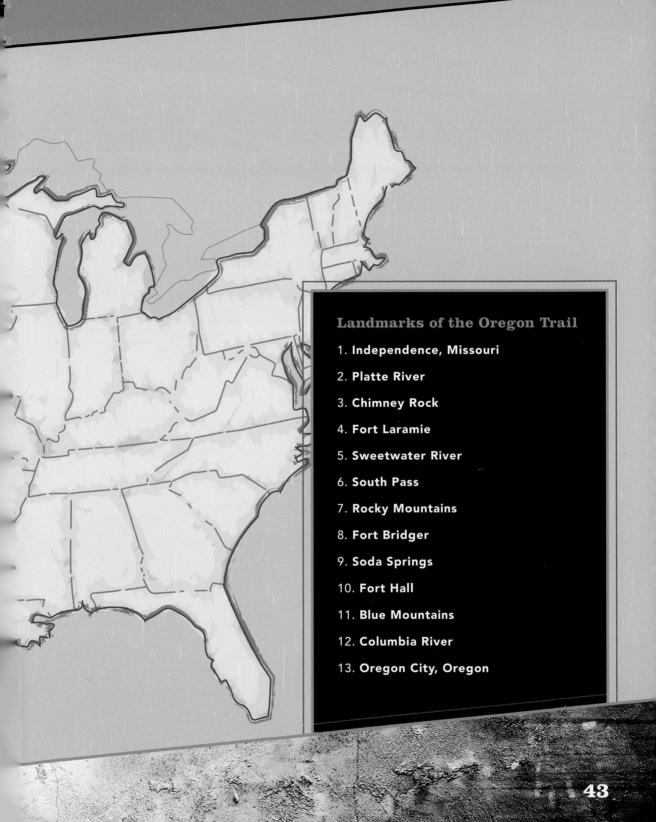

Landmarks of the Oregon Trail

1. **Independence, Missouri**

2. **Platte River**

3. **Chimney Rock**

4. **Fort Laramie**

5. **Sweetwater River**

6. **South Pass**

7. **Rocky Mountains**

8. **Fort Bridger**

9. **Soda Springs**

10. **Fort Hall**

11. **Blue Mountains**

12. **Columbia River**

13. **Oregon City, Oregon**

STOP AND THINK

Tell the Tale

Chapter Two of this book discusses mountain men living in Oregon Country. Imagine you are living as a trapper. Write 200 words about your daily adventures. What types of animals do you see? How will you get through the winter weather?

Surprise Me

Chapter Three talks about the spread of Oregon Fever. After reading this book, what two or three facts about starting out on the Oregon Trail did you find most surprising? Write a few sentences about each fact. Why did you find each fact surprising?

Say What?

Studying the history of the Oregon Trail can mean learning new vocabulary. Find five words in this book you had never heard before. Use a dictionary to find out what they mean. Then write the meanings in your own words. Try using each new word in a sentence.

Dig Deeper

After reading this book, what questions do you still have about the Oregon Trail? Write down one or two questions. With an adult's help, find a few reliable sources that can help answer your questions. Then write a paragraph about what you learned.

GLOSSARY

cholera
a disease often caused by drinking unsafe water

emigrants
people who leave their country to settle in another

fertile
able to produce crops

frontier
a distant part of a country where few people live

landmarks
objects that mark a location

missionaries
people who teach other people about a particular faith

staples
basic food items

terrain
an area of land

territory
an area of land owned by a country that is outside the country's main borders and is not a state

trading posts
places used for buying, selling, or trading goods

transcontinental
going across a continent

tribes
groups of people who have the same language, customs, beliefs, and often the same ancestors

LEARN MORE

Books

Friedman, Mel. *The Oregon Trail.* New York: Children's Press, 2013.

Landau, Elaine. *The Oregon Trail.* New York: Children's Press, 2006.

Young, Frank, and David Lasky. *Oregon Trail: The Road to Destiny.* Seattle, WA: Sasquatch Books, 2011.

Websites

To learn more about the Wild West, visit **booklinks.abdopublishing.com**. These links are routinely monitored and updated to provide the most current information available.

Visit **mycorelibrary.com** for free additional tools for teachers and students.

INDEX

ABOUT THE AUTHOR

Laura K. Murray is the author of more than 30 nonfiction books for children. Her fiction and poetry have appeared in publications such as *The Talking Stick* and *The Lake Region Review*. She lives in North Mankato, Minnesota.